SCHOLASTIC CANADA
BIOGRAPHY

MEET
Terry Fox

ELIZABETH
MacLEOD

ILLUSTRATED BY
MIKE DEAS

Scholastic Canada Ltd.
Toronto New York London Auckland Sydney
Mexico City New Delhi Hong Kong Buenos Aires

The sun was just rising, but Terry Fox had already been running for an hour. Terry took two hops with his left leg, then a long stride with his artificial leg. Step, step, stride. Step, step, stride. Over and over. He clenched his jaw and grimaced in pain.

Up ahead, Terry could see the van where his friend Doug Alward was waiting for him. Terry didn't think about the thousands of kilometres left to go — he just had to make it to the van so he could gulp down some water.

Then Doug would drive ahead a little, and Terry would run again. He was going to run across the whole country to raise money to fight cancer.

3

Terry was born on July 28, 1958, in Winnipeg, Manitoba. Even as a little boy, he was determined. He would carefully stack his wooden blocks. If they fell down, he just piled them up again.

The whole Fox family — Terry; his parents, Betty and Rolly; and his siblings, Fred, Darrell and Judith — loved sports, and they all liked to win. Terry even played table hockey against himself, shooting and playing goalie for both teams.

In 1966, the Fox family moved to Surrey, British Columbia. Two years later, they moved to Port Coquitlam, a city a little east of Vancouver. It was a great place to grow up. The kids picked blueberries in the summers to earn spending money, but Terry still made time for sports.

Terry especially loved basketball — but he wasn't great at first. For one thing, he was shorter than most of the other players. But he tried hard and practised with his friend Doug.

Terry went from being the worst player on his school's team in grade eight to one of the best by grade ten. In grade twelve Terry and Doug shared their school's Athlete of the Year award.

In September 1976, Terry started university. He thought
he might like to be a high-school gym teacher.

Of course, Terry tried out for the university basketball
team. He made it, too. There were other players who had
more talent, but none worked harder than Terry.

7

A few months later, Terry felt a pain in his right knee. He thought it was from playing too much basketball and ignored it. But by early March 1977, the pain was unbearable.

Doctors quickly discovered a type of cancer called osteogenic sarcoma in Terry's knee. They would have to amputate most of his leg right away. That would make sure they got all the cancer cells before they could spread to other parts of his body. Terry cried when he learned the news.

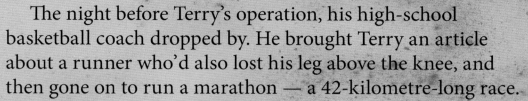

The night before Terry's operation, his high-school basketball coach dropped by. He brought Terry an article about a runner who'd also lost his leg above the knee, and then gone on to run a marathon — a 42-kilometre-long race.

Terry wanted to prove that losing his leg wouldn't stop him. But running one marathon wasn't enough.

Three weeks after Terry's leg was amputated, he tried walking on a prosthetic, or artificial, leg. The stump at the end of his right leg fit into a bucket at the top of the metal leg. Terry found using the new leg really tough, but he kept trying.

Meanwhile, Terry was taking chemotherapy to destroy any cancer cells still in his body. The drugs he was given at the cancer clinic made him feel sick. They also made his hair fall out.

There were many other patients at the clinic. Some of them were in pain or dying. Terry wanted to do something for them. He decided to raise money for cancer research.

11

I SEE THAT KID OUT HERE EVERY DAY.

As soon as he was strong enough, Terry was back playing sports. He was great at wheelchair basketball.

Then, in February 1979, Terry began trying to run. He had to learn to take two steps with his left leg to give his artificial leg time to swing forward. At first he could only cover short distances.

12

Terry trained longer and longer distances every day. Soon his left foot and right stump were covered in blisters and sores. Sometimes they'd start bleeding. But he was still thinking about the marathon runner with one leg.

When most runners finish a marathon, they need lots of time after to recover. Not Terry. He was determined to run a marathon every single day until he'd made it all the way across the country.

IT'S 8530 KILOMETRES, DOUG. THINK I CAN RUN THAT?

WHAT? ALL THE WAY ACROSS CANADA?!

The Canadian Cancer Society agreed to support Terry's run. Terry wrote letters to companies asking for their help too. The businesses offered him running shoes, money, food and even a camper van.

... AND MY PLAN IS TO RUN ACROSS CANADA TO RAISE MONEY FOR CANCER RESEARCH. I'M NOT A DREAMER, BUT I BELIEVE IN MIRACLES. I HAVE TO.

MARATHON OF HOPE
5000 MILES CROSS CANADA
TERRY FOX
MILES TO DATE
MILES TO GO

TERRY FOX - TRANS CANADA RUN
IN AID OF CANCER RESEARCH
FORD AND FUNCRAFT ARE PROUD TO BE ASSOCIATED WITH THIS BRAVE ENDEAVOR

Terry asked his friend Doug to drive the van. Not only did Doug know a lot about running and dealing with injuries, but Terry knew he could depend on him. That would be important in the months ahead.

On April 12, 1980, Terry dipped his artificial leg in the cold, grey waters of the harbour in St. John's, Newfoundland. Then he climbed the steep gravel hill to the road.

The Marathon of Hope had started.

As Terry ran across Newfoundland, people gave him donations as well as meals and sometimes even a place to stay overnight.

Each morning Terry and Doug got up early and were on the road around 4:30 a.m. At the end of the day, Terry carefully marked where he had stopped with a rock. When he started running again the next morning, Terry would touch the marker.

17

Terry ran through strong winds, blazing sun and even a blizzard! But he kept going. Terry ran across Nova Scotia and Prince Edward Island.

Many people still hadn't heard about the Marathon of Hope. Cars and trucks honked at him and sometimes even tried to get him off the road.

In New Brunswick, Terry's brother Darrell joined them. It was fun to have more company.

In some towns, lots of people gave donations. But in others, people still didn't know about Terry's run at all. How was he ever going to reach his goal of raising one dollar for every Canadian?

As Terry crossed from Quebec into Ontario, news of the Marathon of Hope was spreading. People lined the roads to cheer him on, sometimes waiting hours. They pressed money into Terry's hands and thrust bills at Darrell and Doug. They even gave donations to his police escort!

On July 1, Terry stood on his artificial leg and used his left leg to complete the ceremonial kickoff for a Canadian Football League exhibition game in Ottawa. The crowd gave him a standing ovation.

The sun was blazing hot when Terry ran up to a huge rally at Toronto City Hall on July 11. During that one day, Terry raised about $100 000 and got to meet one of his heroes, hockey star Darryl Sittler.

Terry's run exhausted him, but he still made time to meet people along his route. Kids especially inspired Terry. In Terrace Bay, Ontario, he met up with ten-year-old Greg Scott.

Like Terry, Greg loved sports and had lost a leg to bone cancer. He rode his bike behind Terry for almost 10 kilometres and later, they had fun at a nearby lake.

Inspired, Terry was more determined than ever to help.

22

Terry continued to run through Ontario. By September 1, he was outside Thunder Bay. He got up early, as usual, and began his run. But soon Terry started to cough. He felt so bad that he had to lie down in the van.

The coughing stopped, but Terry still felt a strong pain in his neck and chest. So he did what he always did when he was hurting — he kept running.

But Terry quickly realized something was very wrong. He had to stop. Soon he was on his way to the hospital.

Terry had been running for 143 days and had covered 5373 kilometres, or nearly two-thirds of his route across Canada.

Doctors gave Terry the diagnosis he feared: the cancer in his knee had spread to his lungs. He was too sick to keep running. Terry's Marathon of Hope was over.

Terry flew back to Vancouver and went directly into hospital to start chemotherapy again. He was determined to accept the cancer as just another phase in his life.

25

On September 18, 1980, Terry was made a Companion of the Order of Canada. That's the country's highest honour. He was the youngest person ever to earn it.

Three months later, Terry won the Lou Marsh Trophy as Canada's top athlete of the year. That meant a lot to Terry since sports were so important to him.

People kept donating to the Marathon of Hope even after Terry had to stop running. On February 1, 1981, Terry's dream of raising one dollar for every Canadian came true.

But the drugs Terry was taking to fight his cancer weren't working. He was getting weaker and weaker.

On June 28, 1981, Terry died. The whole country mourned the loss of this brave hero

Schools, buildings, parks — even a mountain! — have been named after Terry. Movies have been made about him. A monument stands outside Thunder Bay, near where he had to stop running.

The first Terry Fox Run took place on September 13, 1981. Today, people in thirty countries run, walk and wheel to raise money to fight cancer

Three million Canadian kids participate in Terry Fox School Runs every year. They run in the blazing sun, pouring rain and swirling snow, just as Terry did. Terry's brave and caring spirit lives on in these runs.

Thanks to Terry, more than $780 million has been raised for cancer research. Because of better testing and treatments, today more people with cancer recover than before Terry's run. They can live longer and feel healthier. But there is still lots to do.

Terry believed cancer could be beaten. Many people are still working hard to make his dream come true. And, like Terry, they are determined to succeed.

Terry Fox's Life

July 28, 1958	Terrance Stanley Fox is born in Winnipeg, Manitoba.
1968	Terry's family moves to Port Coquitlam, British Columbia.
March 9, 1977	Terry's right leg is amputated after he is diagnosed with osteogenic sarcoma.
February 1979	Terry starts training for the Marathon of Hope.
April 12, 1980	Terry begins the Marathon of Hope in St. John's, Newfoundland.
September 1, 1980	Terry has to end his run outside Thunder Bay, Ontario, after his cancer returns, this time in his lungs.
September 18, 1980	Terry becomes a Companion of the Order of Canada.
December 18, 1980	Terry is awarded the Lou Marsh Trophy as Canada's top athlete of the year.
February 1, 1981	Terry reaches his goal of raising one dollar for every Canadian, as the Marathon of Hope fund climbs to $24,170,000 with donations still coming in.

TERRY AND DOUG IN HOWLEY, NEWFOUNDLAND.

EVERY STEP WAS TOUGH FOR TERRY -- YOU CAN SEE THE DETERMINATION ON HIS FACE.

June 28, 1981	Terry dies of metastatic osteogenic sarcoma in New Westminster, British Columbia.
July 17, 1981	A peak in the Rocky Mountains is named Mount Terry Fox.
August 29, 1981	Terry is elected to Canada's Sports Hall of Fame.
September 13, 1981	The first Terry Fox Run is held. About 300 000 people across Canada raise $3.5 million to fight cancer.
April 13, 1982	The first Terry Fox stamp is issued by Canada Post. (Another was released in 2000 and a third in 2017.)
May 26, 1988	The Terry Fox Foundation is set up to raise and distribute money in Terry's name for cancer research.
June 30, 1999	Terry is voted Canada's Greatest Hero.
April 4, 2005	A loonie with Terry's image on it is released.
September 27, 2014	Terry is awarded the Order of the Sash by the Métis Nation British Columbia.

THE CANADA 150 MARATHON OF HOPE STAMP.

WITH TERRY ARE (FROM LEFT) FATHER ROLLY, BROTHER DARRELL, MOTHER BETTY AND SISTER JUDITH IN JULY, 1980.

TERRY LOVED HAVING A CHANCE TO RELAX, EAT AND TALK WITH PEOPLE HE MET DURING HIS RUN.

31

For more information about Terry and the Terry Fox Run, please visit www.terryfox.org.

Dedicated to Jackson Kyleman and Wyatt Coleman on behalf of your grandmother, Kathy.
May you have Terry Fox's courage, determination and sense of purpose.
"Dreams are made possible if you try."
— E.M.

For the Terry Fox Foundation and all of the positive work they do
— M.D.

It is an honour to write about such a great Canadian hero. Thank you to everyone on the Scholastic team for giving me this opportunity. Special thanks to amazing editor Erin O'Connor, fabulous illustrator Mike Deas and wonderful designer Andrea Casault. Many, many thanks to Darrell Fox, senior adviser and board member of the Terry Fox Research Institute and Terry Fox Foundation member, for reviewing the manuscript and illustrations. I'm also very grateful to Terry's other siblings, Fred Fox and Judith Fox-Alder, for commenting on the manuscript. I appreciate Kathy Coleman's support of this book. Thank you to my brothers, John and Douglas, and special thanks to Paul for his help with research and for being there for the long run.
— E.M.

Scholastic Canada Ltd.
604 King Street West, Toronto, Ontario M5V 1E1, Canada

Scholastic Inc.
557 Broadway, New York, NY 10012, USA

Scholastic Australia Pty Limited
PO Box 579, Gosford, NSW 2250, Australia

Scholastic New Zealand Limited
Private Bag 94407, Botany, Manukau 2163, New Zealand

Scholastic Children's Books
Euston House, 24 Eversholt Street, London NW1 1DB, UK

www.scholastic.ca

The illustrations were created using a blend of digital tools with traditional media. Sketches were created with a Wacom tablet and Photoshop, then traced onto watercolour paper, where colour and texture were added using gouache and watercolour paints. Ink was used to add the black line to finish the art.

Photos ©: title and cover pages speech bubble, top right: fatmayilmaz/iStockphoto;

Photos ©: 30 left: Darryl Kelly; 30 right: Gail Harvey; 31 left: Colin McConnell/Toronto Star via Getty Images; top right: Courtesy Canada Post; 31 bottom right: Boris Spremo/Toronto Star via Getty Images. With thanks to Christine Kelly and family.

Library and Archives Canada Cataloguing in Publication
Title: Meet Terry Fox / Elizabeth MacLeod ; illustrated by Mike Deas.
Names: MacLeod, Elizabeth, author. | Deas, Mike, 1982- illustrator.
Description: Series statement: Scholastic Canada biography
Identifiers: Canadiana 20190177454 | ISBN 9781443182072 (softcover) | ISBN 9781443182065 (hardcover)Subjects: LCSH: Fox, Terry, 1958-1981. | LCSH: Cancer—Patients—Canada—Biography—Juvenile literature. | LCSH: Runners (Sports)—Canada—Biography—Juvenile literature. | LCGFT: Biographies.
Classification: LCC RC265.6.F68 M33 2020 | DDC j362.196/9940092—dc23

6 5 4 3 2 1   Printed in Malaysia 108   20 21 22 23 24

MEET TERRY FOX, THE YOUNG ATHLETE WITH A VISION THAT INSPIRED PEOPLE AROUND THE WORLD.

Growing up, Terry Fox loved sports. Whether it was basketball, volleyball or track and field, he gave it his all. It was a terrible day when, at only 18, he was diagnosed with bone cancer. His right leg was amputated above the knee.

But Terry never gave up. He decided to run across Canada to raise awareness and money for cancer research. Terry trained hard and on April 12, 1980, he began the Marathon of Hope.

Then, 5373 kilometres into his run, Terry was forced to stop — but his incredible legacy was just beginning.

Also available in the Scholastic Canada Biography series: *Meet Viola Desmond, Meet Chris Hadfield, Meet Tom Longboat, Meet Elsie MacGill* and *Meet Willie O'Ree.*

ISBN 978-1-4431-8207-2

9 781443 182072

90000

Scholastic Canada Ltd.

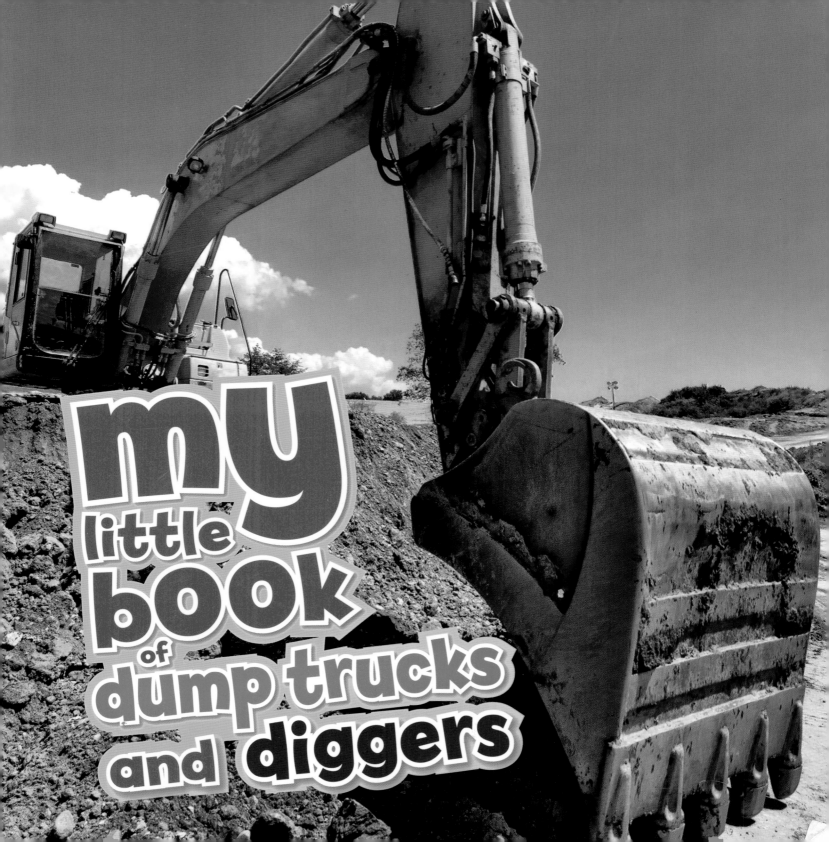

my little book of dump trucks and diggers